Coyote Tales

COYOTE TALES

Adapted by Hettie Jones   Illustrated by Louis Mofsie

Holt, Rinehart and Winston · New York Chicago San Francisco

Library of Congress Cataloging in Publication Data

Jones, Hettie.
Coyote tales.
SUMMARY: Stories adapted from Assiniboine, Skidi, Pawnee, and Dakota legends.
CONTENTS: Coyote steals the summer.—Coyote loses his dinner.
—Coyote rescues the ring-girl.—Coyote conquers the Iya.
1. Assiniboine Indians—Legends. 2. Pawnee Indians—Legends. 3. Dakota Indians—Legends.
[1. Indians of North America—Legends] I. Mofsie, Louis, illus. II. Title.

E99.A84J66   398.2'09701 [398.2]   73-17400

ISBN 0-03-088346-6

Printed in the United States of America
Designed by Robert Reed.
First Edition

No TOC

Contents

INTRODUCTION

Coyote the trickster is a familiar figure in the lore of all the American Indian tribes who, at one time or another, lived on the Great Plains. The stories here are adapted from legends known among the Assiniboine, Dakota, and Skidi Pawnee people; they are similar to some told by the Blackfoot, Crow, Cree, Arapaho, and others.

Coyote is an enigma, always on the move, hungry most of the time, and forever transforming himself into something else. Most often he appears as an old man or a coyote, but he can change himself into anything else at will. He amuses himself by getting into trouble, usually for the purpose of tricking another out of some food.

Besides being a trickster, Coyote is one of the creative spirits. He has many names—Na'pi or Old Man, Wi'hio, and Iktomi are only a few of them. The Hidatsa call him "First-worker," because, during the formation of the world, he did a great deal to make it a good place in which to live. He was also the founder of certain customs and beliefs.

But most of the time Coyote is out to play tricks on all the other animals, and on people as well. His improbable tales—*ohu'kaka* as they are called by the Dakota—are intended for the amusement of young and old. The stories are as different as the people who tell them: some are pornographic; others are long, rambling adventures; still others account for the way things are. The four in this book were adapted from material collected by nineteenth- and twentieth-century anthropologists. In the first, Coyote receives his powers of trickery from the Sky Spirit in exchange for bringing summer to a frost-bound earth. In the second, because he doesn't always win, Coyote loses his tasty dinner to the crafty Fox. The third story shows him at his best, tricking a young girl into calling out the buffalo for him to hunt, and at his worst, when he can't shoot a single one. In the last story, unusual because Coyote appears in the role of helper, he conquers a huge man-eating monster, and thereby gains the favor of all.

No matter what he is doing, though, Coyote is there to be laughed at. Whatever his name or form, he is ridiculous, sometimes outrageous, a winner and a loser too. At the end of each story he disappears, which is also part of his charm. For the joy of Coyote is his nonchalance and detachment, and his appearances are all the more delightful because they are never expected. Coyote is always surprising; no one ever knows where he will turn up next, or in what form, or where he's been. He's always just "going along." Like the old men who used to go from village to village to tell his stories, he merely turns up, and gives everyone a good laugh before he leaves.

Coyote Tales

COYOTE STEALS THE SUMMER

Once it was winter all the time over most of the earth. Snow lay deep on the ground. The animals stayed cold. Nothing grew. Many were hungry. The Sky Spirit knew who was keeping the summer, but so far, he had been unable to get it back. One day he decided to ask Coyote's help, and called him up to the sky.

"If you can get rid of winter, you will be given the power to fool people and the power to make anything talk except water," the spirit promised.

"But is it possible to get rid of winter?" Coyote asked. "It's been like this for so long. . . ."

"Far to the east," the spirit explained, "there's a man who keeps the summer tied to one of the poles of his tipi."

"Has anyone tried to steal it?" asked Coyote.

"Yes, but so far no one has been able to. The man has powers. He can tell when anyone approaches his tipi."

Coyote thought for a while. "It would be nice to have the power to fool people and the power to make things talk," he said. Then he declared he would get the summer, and he left the sky.

At night the earth was so cold Coyote couldn't sleep. He dug in the snow-covered ground looking for sticks with which to build a fire. "It certainly would help if we weren't always freezing," he thought, as he struck up a flame. "Ah, that's better."

He crouched near the flames and thought of ways to steal the summer. Then he noticed a small white shape among the shadows. Rabbit, in her winter coat, had come to get warm. Suddenly Coyote got an idea: she, with a few others, would be helpers. Together, they could get the summer back. He jumped up. "Little sister," he called, "come closer, it feels good."

"Thank you," said Rabbit gratefully, hopping to the fire.

Coyote watched as she first turned one ear and then the other to catch the warmth. "Are there any other animals around here, little one?" he asked.

"Yes, there are," Rabbit answered dreamily. enjoying the warmth.

"Who?"

"Who?" echoed Rabbit, gazing at the fire. "Let's see, there's Wolf, and Fox, and some of the birds . . ."

"Birds too, eh? That's fine, fine. Little sister," Coyote continued, "would you ask them to come to me? I have something important to tell everyone."

Rabbit, sure that her friends would appreciate the fire, hopped away and soon returned with the others, who hastened to the fire to warm themselves.

"What was the something important you had to tell us?" Fox asked, smiling pleasantly in Coyote's direction.

Coyote smiled back at her slyly and made his announcement. "Little ones, we are going to look for the summer, steal it, and bring it here, to this country."

They stared at him. "What's the summer?" Hawk asked.

"Don't ask questions," Coyote answered. "Just do what I tell you, and it will be good for us." He began to stamp out the fire.

"But . . . must we go right *now*?" Fox protested. "Just when we've finally gotten warm?" She looked at Wolf and Rabbit, and then at the birds. Everyone seemed as confused as she.

"Who is going where? And when?" asked Wolf, glaring at Rabbit as though it were all her fault. "You never said——"

"I said no more questions!" Coyote barked. Since they all appeared quite offended, he added in a gentler tone: "We're going east to the end of the snow, and we'll start tonight!" He kicked at the fire one last time. Then, after a look at the sky to get his direction, he began walking quickly toward the east.

Not knowing what else to do, the others followed. "Now don't blame it all on me," said Rabbit to the grumpy Wolf as they trudged along in the darkness behind Coyote. "I just thought you'd enjoy the fire."

Wolf just grunted in annoyance.

"The fire was fine," Fox put in, "but what comes next?"

"He said it would be good for us," Owl reminded them, flying low to catch the conversation.

Wolf shrugged. "It's easy for you to talk. You're not walking," he muttered, and turned his nose to the road ahead.

They traveled for months. When they finally arrived at the snow's edge, Coyote set up a high pole and asked fast-flying Hawk to perch on it. A short distance away, on the summer ground, they could see the back of a large tipi. Coyote ordered Rabbit and Wolf to stand in a line between the pole and the tipi.

"And what are Owl and I supposed to do?" asked Fox. "Stand here and stare at the snow?"

"You'll soon have something to do, don't worry," Coyote said. "First, Owl, you fly up quietly to that tipi's smoke-hole and peek down.

Find out if the summer is tied up anywhere inside, but don't let the owner see you!"

Owl flew to the tipi, lit on the smoke-hole without a sound, and looked down.

"What are you doing here!" the owner cried, looking up. He threw a blazing piece of wood at Owl, hitting him on the nose.

Poor burned Owl flew back to report. While Rabbit applied snow to the injury, Owl told Coyote that the owner had tied a bag to one of the tipi poles. "I thig it was the subber," he said, sniffling through his hurt nose. "Anyway, it was a sball skin bag."

"Very good," said Coyote. "We needed you because you fly so quietly. Now go take care of your nose, and we'll take care of the rest." He put on a long fox-skin breechclout and tied it around his waist. It hung to the ground. He beckoned to Fox. "Now it's your turn. Follow me. I'm going over to the tipi. If you walk right behind my legs, no one will be able to see you."

Silently they crept to the tipi, but as they came near, a voice called out, "Who's there? Is that Owl back again?"

Coyote whispered, "Fox, crawl in here and pull the summer down from its pole. When you come out, run between my legs toward the others —fast—and pass the bag to the next in line."

Coyote waited as Fox crawled in. A few seconds later she came charging out, the bag in her mouth and the owner at her heels. She dashed between Coyote's outspread legs. The owner, reaching for her, caught hold of the fox-skin breechclout instead. To fool him, Coyote grabbed it too, yelling, "I've got her, I've got her." Both he and the owner fell on top of the skin.

Then the owner turned the skin over and saw that it was empty. "Get up, you must be sitting on her!" he shouted at Coyote.

"No, I'm sure I caught her!" Coyote shouted

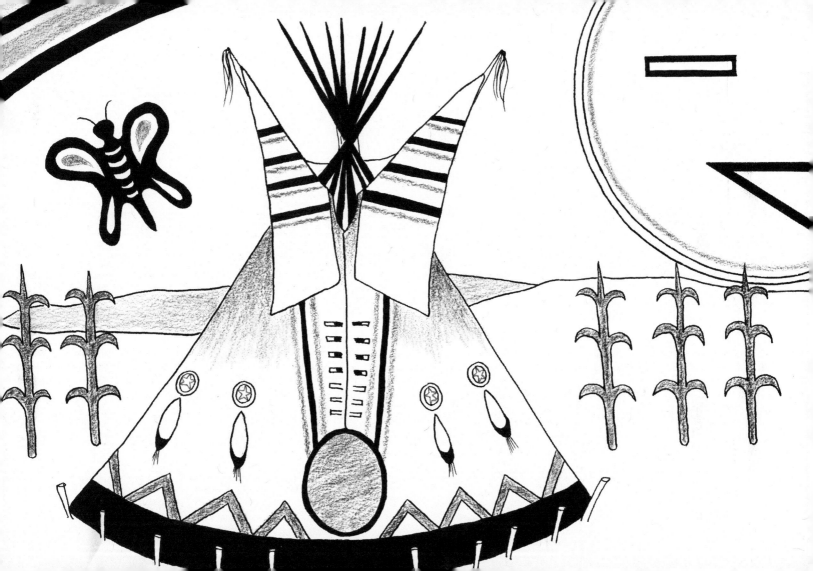

back. "Wait—maybe she went underground—what's in that hole over there?"

The owner looked but of course found nothing. "Well, let's think about it," said sly Coyote. "I have my pipe here. Why don't we sit down and smoke and consider the matter?"

Suddenly, the distracted owner caught sight of Fox passing the bag to Wolf. "There she is! That Wolf has her! Stop, thief!" He took off after Wolf, but Wolf had already passed the bag to Rabbit.

"Now I'll get you!" The owner made a mad dash for Rabbit, but she hopped over to the snow where she was practically invisible in her winter coat, and soon she was at the pole. Ready now to do his part, Hawk flew down from his perch, took the summer in his mouth, and soared away with it.

"Come back here, you—you big bird!" the owner cried. "Oh, now they have it for sure. What can I do? Oh, my summer!" The cold had set in and he started to shiver. "Oh, I'm freezing, I'd better go home." He turned toward his tipi and came face to face with Coyote.

Tricky Coyote had sprinkled water on his face, pretending to be perspired from his efforts. "I tried to get that Fox," he panted, "but I never even saw her. Did you catch her?"

The owner replied that yes, he'd seen her; no, he hadn't caught her. And what's more, he had had to chase Wolf, Rabbit, and Hawk as well. Coyote pretended to grow very angry. He tore up the earth with his knife, even threatened to kill the thieves with it. "Let's track them down," he urged.

"No," said the owner, his teeth chattering. "It's getting too c-c-cold for me without the summer. I'm not used to it. I have to get inside. Will you c-c-catch them for me?"

"I will certainly go right after them," Coyote

promised. "I'm sure that soon your precious summer will be safely in my hands." He turned to go. A tricky smile lit up his face as he reflected on the power he had. Fooling people was as much fun as making things talk.

"Brothers and sisters, we've done it!" Coyote greeted the others. Hawk circled slowly overhead, the summer still in his bill. "You can bring that bag down now," Coyote called up to him.

Everyone stood around watching as Coyote untied it. No one knew what would happen when the bag was opened. They grew silent with delight as gradually the snow disappeared and they found themselves standing on warm, sweet earth. All about them were buds and leaves sprouting from the trees.

"We bust have the right bag," said Owl finally. "The air feels just like it did over there where old dose-hitter lives."

Wolf rolled over on his back, feeling the new grass grow under him. "This feels so good," he sighed.

"Yes, the weather's fine," Rabbit agreed, "but I'm not really dressed for it. I feel peculiar."

"You do look a little out of place in that white coat," Fox commented, looking her over.

Rabbit's nose was twitching. "I feel ridiculous. I'll just have to change my coat."

"I wouldn't bother doing that," warned Coyote, who was busy tying up the bag again, "because we've got to carry this home."

As soon as the bag was tied they felt the cold again. In a few minutes a heavy snow was falling. It soon covered the ground. Everyone looked miserable, groping their way through the storm.

"It was too good to last," murmured Rabbit resentfully. "Now I'll never get to wear my brown coat, never!"

"I certainly hope you're wrong," Fox said.

Turning to Wolf who was floundering beside her in a large drift, she hinted loudly so that Coyote would overhear, "Don't you think you might like walking better during the *summer*???"

"Wait a minute, little sister, I'll do something." Coyote reopened the bag, strewing summer along their path. It was lovely at first, but after a while Wolf and Fox complained that their feet tired easily walking on the hard ground. So, Coyote made snow again. "Let me know when your feet get tender and I'll change off," he said. They went along, walking first in summer, then in winter, with Coyote changing the weather as they went. It was winter when they came to their own country.

"Now bay we please have subber for a good, long time?" asked Owl. "I deed a rest."

"No, now we are going to take this bag up to the sky," Coyote declared, paying no attention to the grumbles and sighs that greeted his latest order.

In the sky, the spirit thanked them and sent for all the creatures of the earth. "I will ask each one what kind of weather he prefers, and for how long a time. Right now, though, it shall be summer."

"A wise decision," Owl said.

It was a lovely morning when the beasts and birds arrived. Coyote told Rabbit she looked beautiful in her new brown coat. They all seemed to be enjoying the good weather. But Frost was among them. He wasn't as happy as the others because he kept melting.

The Sky Spirit called the meeting to order. "First we will hear everyone's opinion, then Coyote will judge," he announced.

Bear spoke first. He'd been asleep for such a long time that he was still groggy. "Let the winter last forty months," he said with a yawn.

"No!" Deer stamped her foot in disagreement. "We've just *had* a long winter. We need the nice, warm weather for a while."

Raccoon felt that there shouldn't be any winter at all. In a long speech he gave the reasons why. He went on and on.

"Be quiet or you'll have to leave," Coyote interrupted him finally. "You're as bad as the man from whom we just stole this summer."

"You ought to have winter at least part of the time," Frost suggested. "Summer forever might get boring. Everyone needs a change."

Rabbit thought Frost was very understanding. Though she loved her brown coat, she just knew she'd want to wear the white one again someday. Fox mentioned that she personally would like to see snow for part of the year. "It's softer when you have to do a lot of walking," she explained. Wolf agreed, and a few more offered their opinions.

Frog was the last to speak. Puffing on his pipe, he stated thoughtfully: "Let there be six months of winter and six months of summer."

At this Coyote snatched up a club and hit Frog over the head for no reason at all. "That is too short a time for each season," he yelled.

Everyone laughed. Frog looked so funny that Coyote laughed too and helped him sit up again. Coyote put on a serious face. "You are right after all, Frog. It shall be as you say." He turned to the others.

"Ahem! If the discussion is over, I shall judge the best way I know how. Six months of winter and six months of summer, as Frog suggested. That is the best way. Now Frost, you must go far north and stay there for the next six months. When winter comes, you may return, and then you will be in charge. You may make some days of cold weather, but don't make it too cold or we'll bring you back up here to the sky and not allow any winter at all."

"Fine," Frost agreed. "I'm going right this minute while there's still some of me left."

Everyone else eagerly departed for earth. Once there, Coyote made them all stop to jump into a hole full of fat. They lined up in single file.

"What's holding us up now?" complained Wolf, standing at the end of the line. "Come on—I'm in a hurry to get back home."

"It's important," Coyote explained. "If we get this into our bodies every summer, we'll keep warm for the six months of winter."

Wolf looked doubtful. "Don't you think we should eat it instead?" he asked.

Rabbit came running over. "My coat," she said breathlessly, "will it be good for my coat?"

"Absolutely," Coyote assured her. "It's the best thing you can do."

"I still think eating it is better," Wolf groaned, but he jumped in anyway, and Rabbit jumped in after him.

"Good," said Coyote as he slid through the hole. "Now that is done." And he went along.

COYOTE LOSES HIS DINNER

Coyote was so hungry he could hardly walk. He dragged himself up the steep hill he had decided to climb and looked down from the top. A large flock of geese was feeding at the edge of a lake below.

"What luck!" Coyote sat down to rest and planned how he would trick them. "First I'll pretend to be in mourning." Taking his knife, he scratched himself in various places and cut off his hair. Then he picked up a large stick, and leaning heavily on it, made his way slowly down the hill.

To the geese he appeared to be someone bent over with sorrow. As he drew near they noticed he was crying. "What's the matter?" one asked. Soon all the others stopped eating and came to investigate.

Coyote sat down in the grass. "My brother has been killed," he answered between sobs. "I am out to revenge his death, and I don't care if I get killed myself." He wailed mightily, making as much noise as possible. "Last night, I dreamed that by the shore of a big lake I would find my brothers the geese. And I dreamed———" he raised his voice to a shout, "that they would join my war party."

The geese began to honk excitedly, for they were not often included in such an effort. When their chief came forward to ask if all this were true, Coyote repeated his story.

"But I want only the biggest and fattest of your tribe to come," he added slyly. "I don't want any weak geese fighting on my side."

"That is agreed," said the chief. "I will even

accompany you myself."

"Good," said Coyote. "Before we start, though, we should hold a dance here. I'll show you how."

Since the geese were extremely curious, Coyote could do exactly as he pleased with them. In the outermost circle he placed those with the fattest breasts. Inside in the next ring he put the next best, and so on, until four circles were formed. Then he warned them: "This dance has a special rule which you must not break, or we won't be able to perform it. Will you obey?"

"Of course," said the silly geese.

"Well then, while I am singing, you must dance with your eyes closed. If you open your eyes for any reason, they will turn red."

The geese closed their eyes. Coyote beat his drum and began singing:

Dance with your eyes closed,

No red eye, shall we spy,
Dance with your eyes closed.

The geese danced on with their eyes closed. It was quite a sight. As they danced, Coyote walked around chanting, "Dance with your eyes closed," killing each goose in the first circle by wringing its neck. "No red eye, shall we spy," Coyote sang as he killed all the geese in the second circle. On and on he chanted, until soon all the geese in the third circle were dead. "No red eye, shall we . . ."

Suddenly one of the dancers in the last circle stumbled on a stone and accidentally opened his eyes. Seeing his dead brothers, he ran for the lake, screaming to those who were left, "Run! Run for your lives! Coyote is killing us all!"

The geese fled, honking fearfully and flapping their wings until they were well out over the lake where Coyote couldn't reach them. But Coyote didn't care. "Don't worry," he called, "I don't want any more of you—I've got enough here!" He set to work tying up his prey, feeling very pleased with himself.

With the geese slung over his shoulder, Coyote walked along looking for a good place to have his feast. He was delighted to find a pleasant clearing full of soft, thick grass where he built a fire. He put some of the geese up on spits; the rest he covered with hot ashes. Soon a delicious aroma filled the clearing. Coyote, his mouth watering, lay down to rest until the food was ready.

He definitely wasn't planning to have company for dinner. But the good smell wafted through the woods like an invitation, and soon Fox arrived at the edge of the woods and stood peeking through the trees. Knowing how tricky Coyote was and seeing the geese, she decided it would be fun to outtrick Coyote. First she bandaged one of her legs, making it look horribly swollen. Then she waited until the geese were done and hobbled into the clearing, leaning on a stick and looking as miserable as she dared.

Coyote jumped in alarm, but noticing Fox's injured leg he said kindly, "Come here, my poor little sister."

Fox dragged herself to the fire and lay down panting. She gazed hungrily at the geese. Coyote, seeing her hungry glances, covered his food with leaves. Then he tried to change the subject. "Little sister, how did you hurt your leg?" he asked.

"I fell jumping over some rocks when I was out looking for food," answered Fox, tears gathering in her eyes.

Though Coyote felt sorry for her, he never gave up a good meal easily. "If you really want my geese, little sister," he said slyly, "why don't we race for them? Once around the lake—whoever wins gets the geese."

"But my leg," Fox whined pitifully. "I

couldn't possibly run. I'm not even sure I can get up!"

Now that was a different problem to consider. Coyote knew he had to get Fox out of the clearing—why, he wouldn't be able to eat a bite with her sitting there watching him! "I'll tie a big stone to my foot and then we'll be even," he offered.

"I think even a stone-tied leg can beat this bad one of mine," sighed Fox, "but that is very generous of you. I'll run then, even though my leg hurts." Grasping the stick, she pulled herself to her feet and managed a few limping steps.

"What a race this is going to be," Coyote thought, observing Fox's condition. "Poor little sister doesn't look able to run past the next tree." As he looked for and found a suitable stone, he felt rather sorry for her. And so he told Fox she could have a head start.

Leaving Coyote to tie on the stone, Fox went limping away slowly. As soon as she was hidden by the woods, she tore off the bandage and raced away. Keeping to the woods, she ran all around the lake back to the clearing.

Ah, how delicious those geese were! She ate all of them down to the bone. "Mmmm, that Coyote's a fine cook—I must remember to tell him," Fox laughed. "But not right now," she added, hearing a noise not too far away. "Right now I'd better get out of here!" Hastily she covered over all the bones with leaves and hid.

Moments later Coyote crashed into the clearing. With a sigh of relief he threw himself down in the soft grass, untied the stone and irritably tossed it into the bushes. "It's terrible," he said, rubbing his ankle. "I had to go through all this just to eat my own dinner, and now I'm almost too tired. . . . But I may as well get started"—he reached under the leaves—"or that Fox will be back limping around and looking pitiful, trying to . . ." His voice trailed off as he gazed at the bone he had pulled out. He stared at it as though it were something difficult to recognize. "Oh," he said finally, "a bone." And then, "Someone must have eaten one of my geese." He threw the bone over his shoulder and, reaching in again, grabbed another. "More bones!" He jumped up and frantically dug through the leaves.

"All bones!" He kicked at them. "Nothing but bones! All my geese . . . that Fox . . . I've been tricked!" In a fury Coyote ran howling through the woods down to the lake, calling for Fox to appear and swearing to do away with her.

On the opposite side stood Fox, grinning and patting her full stomach. "Coyote!" She waved and bounded down to the shore with no trace of a limp. "Thanks for dinner, little brother! It was delicious. You're a fine cook!"

"Come back here, Fox . . . you . . . you-oooo . . . " Coyote's voice rose in a howl.

"You think you can fool everyone, but this time I fooled you, *little brother*," Fox teased.

"No one can fool me and get away with it," Coyote cried.

"But I did!" Fox shouted triumphantly as she disappeared through the trees. "And one day you may even be fooled again!"

"Never!" yelled Coyote. "No one will ever fool me again!"

And still hungry, he went along.

COYOTE RESCUES THE RING-GIRL

Long ago, there was a girl who lived on the plains with her four brothers in a very big earth lodge. She was kept inside most of the time because she had the power to attract buffalo.

Her brothers used her whenever they wanted to hunt buffalo. First they would be sure to have plenty of arrows, which they made from dogwood sticks, flint stones, and feathers gathered in the woods nearby. Then they would call their sister to come and sit in a swing that hung outside the lodge. They swung her gently, not too high, but high enough for the buffalo to see her. As soon as dust appeared on the horizon they knew the buffalo were coming. One of the boys would quickly take his sister inside. She would climb into a skin bag attached by ropes to the tallest lodge pole, and

he would hoist her to the top of the pole and tie the string at the bottom. This way she was safe, for not only were the buffalo attracted to her, they also wanted to carry her away to their own country.

In those days buffalo were numerous. The brothers had been able to kill many each time they swung their sister, and the big lodge was usually crowded with bags full of meat.

One morning the boys went somewhere. While they were gone Coyote, who knew about the girl's power, came to visit. Hungry as usual, he planned a buffalo hunt for himself, which he began to arrange as soon as she appeared at the door.

"Granddaughter," he whined, "I'm so hun-

gry. I must have something to eat. Will you give me some meat, please?"

"Grandfather, there is plenty. You shall have all you want," the girl answered kindly. She roasted some dried meat and softened it with melted fat. This she offered to Coyote, who was sunning himself in a patch of long grass near the swing, thinking about how to get her into it.

"No, granddaughter," he said sadly, waving away the food she held out. "No, I really don't think I'd be able to eat that. It's too hard and dry for this old grandfather. My teeth, you know . . ." He glanced hungrily at the meat and then, his eyes on the girl, said in a low voice, "Could you perhaps make it a little softer?"

"Poor grandfather. I'll try." She couldn't help feeling sorry for him. She got out her mortar and ground the meat with a pestle, adding more fat. But when this was brought to Coyote, he again refused. Now he had to have fresh meat.

"We have some that my brothers cut up just before they left," the girl said. She had begun to wonder just what he did want.

"No, that kind is still too dry for me. I can only eat fresh-killed meat." Coyote sighed and looked at her pleadingly. "Do you think you might sit in the swing for a while? I'd be so grateful if you'd let me swing you, just for a little while?"

"Oh no, I couldn't do that," she protested. No one other than her brothers had ever swung her.

"I have plenty of arrows with me," Coyote assured her, pointing to his full quiver, "and though I've never done it, I'm certain I can kill buffalo."

The girl hesitated. "Grandfather, I don't think . . ." She stood in the doorway looking doubtfully at him.

"Please?" Coyote whimpered. "I'm so hungry. . . ."

"You'd better wait until my brothers come home, because only they know exactly how to push the swing." She was afraid to trust him. "Besides, one person alone could never manage it— what if the buffalo were to find me?"

But Coyote insisted, promising to swing her gently, not too high, and to help her hide in the skin bag. He swore he would do everything correctly. Finally she agreed, though not without some misgivings. "Now make sure you don't push too hard," she reminded, as he helped her into the swing. "My brothers will be very angry if anything happens to me."

Coyote arranged his arrows. The girl sat worrying while he fixed his bowstring and tied his wrist protector in place. Then slowly he pushed the swing. Nothing happened. Slowly he pushed again. "I wonder how long it takes," he thought, beginning to push a little harder. Alarmed, the girl called down that he had promised to swing her gently. But Coyote didn't answer. His attention was elsewhere. He had just seen dust on the horizon! He pushed harder and harder. As the swing flew even higher, the girl held on for her life, shouting helplessly for him to stop!

All at once buffalo came charging at them from every direction. Coyote shot wildly; not a single arrow hit its mark. In a moment the huge snorting beasts had surrounded him, stamping and pushing him aside in their eagerness to get at the girl. Terrified, Coyote dropped his bow and arrows and fled to a creek near the lodge. From the mud where he hid, he could hear the cries of the girl, as she was carried off to buffalo country on the horns of the largest bull.

Not until the last buffalo had disappeared over the hills did Coyote leave his hiding place.

His bow and arrows were torn to bits and lay strewn all over the ground. The swing dangled from its broken ropes, swaying emptily in the breeze. Coyote felt ashamed and then disgusted, because he had no idea what to do next. He buried himself in the mud again, waiting.

Before long the boys returned. They knew at once what had happened; someone had coaxed her to swing, but who? When Coyote came up from his hole all covered with mud and hanging his head, they grabbed him and threw him to the ground.

"So it was you!" Four angry faces glared down at him.

Coyote closed his eyes. "Grandchildren, let me up, let me up," he whined, but they held him fast. Someone shook the broken quiver over his face.

"Why did you do this to her?" the eldest brother demanded. Coyote trembled. He stopped struggling and tried to explain.

"All I did was ask your sister for something to eat, but you know your poor grandfather is getting old and can't eat dry meat, so I asked her to swing. . . . I—I tried to kill the buffalo but they didn't seem to care for my arrows . . . nearly ran over me . . . I dropped my bow . . ."

"And then?"

Coyote opened the other eye. All the angry faces were still there. ". . . and, um, and . . . and then I hid down at the creek," he confessed.

"You left her alone . . . you let them take her!" The brothers were furious; the second youngest, a warrior, threatened Coyote with a terrible death.

"No, no," he begged, trying desperately to think of some way out. "Don't kill me . . . if you let me live I'll go after her today, to buffalo country, and bring her back to you tomorrow."

"That's only right," said the eldest. "He

should have a chance to bring her back. Release him."

Coyote sprang up, ready to run. "I'll *surely* get her," he said, backing away. He had no idea how he was going to accomplish this.

"One day only," warned the second youngest brother. "If you fail, we will *surely* kill you—and you know how." Coyote shuddered and fled. The brothers let him go, hoping he would keep his word. They knew they could always find him if he didn't.

In the long afternoon shadows Coyote was still running. At the edge of a wood he came upon Rusty-Blackbird, who asked where he was going in such a hurry and why didn't he stop a minute.

"Is there anyone chasing me?" Coyote gasped.

"No, not that I can see," said Rusty-Blackbird.

"Oh, then maybe I'll rest." Coyote sank down wearily in the grass and told Rusty-Blackbird the whole story, explaining that he was now on his way to rescue the girl from the buffalo. The bird listened thoughtfully.

"You know, I wouldn't mind joining you," he offered, "that is, if you'd care for company."

Deciding immediately that a helper might be useful, Coyote told Rusty-Blackbird that it would be fine if he came along. They traveled until just after sunset, when they came to a tall tree. Coyote asked the bird to perch at its very top. "This is about halfway," he said. "Stay here tonight and wait for me. I'll go get the girl and then tomorrow you can carry her the rest of the way back to her brothers."

Rusty-Blackbird agreed, thinking that might be fun. Coyote was delighted. He had *not* wanted to look that second youngest brother in the eye at all, with or without the girl. He trotted along happily under a brilliant moon until he met Hawk, who was out doing a little night-flying. When Coyote told him the story, Hawk also wanted to help.

"Good," said Coyote, "come on." The more of them, the easier for me, he thought. He and Hawk traveled together until the stars had gone out and the sky was a light, faded gray. When they came to a tree and Coyote deposited Hawk on it, the bird ruffled his feathers and sat down on a branch, looking annoyed.

"I wanted to go with you," he complained. "Here I've been flying all night, and now you won't let me come along!"

"But this way you'll get some rest," Coyote explained. "I'll bring the girl to you, then you fly with her to Rusty-Blackbird. It's easier."

"Easier for whom?" Hawk snapped. He didn't like waiting in trees all day but he'd do it anyway, he said, if it wouldn't take too long, so Coyote had

better get going. Coyote sniffed and ran off, thinking how much he would prefer sitting in a tree all day to chasing all over buffalo country. Still, he decided, having help was a good idea even if some of them complained; and on the way, he even persuaded first Wolf and then Badger to join the rescue team. He left them both at sunrise on a grassy hill that overlooked the buffalo's village. Below, on a large dusty field, the buffalo were playing an early-morning game with sticks and a ring.

When Coyote came down the hill they were all lined up at the south end of the field. Since the girl was nowhere in sight and he was tired anyway, he sat down at the north end to watch the game.

Two buffalo held sticks and one of them also held the ring. They began running toward the north end of the field. The one with the ring tossed

it far and high, then both hurled their sticks at it to see whose would go through first. At the north end, they picked up the sticks and the ring and played in the other direction. When the first players were done, two others had a turn.

The second players, nearing Coyote, shouted at him to get out of the way. He rose, and after limping around a bit, sat down again, close to the end of the field. He was curious. There was something about that ring. Coyote looked hard. The sticks seemed peculiarly drawn to it. He watched a while longer, wondering if this were all his imagination, then decided it was worth a try. The next time the players came by, the ring rolled past him. Quickly he whispered to it, "Granddaughter, I am here to save you. When they throw you, run to me, and I will take you home to your brothers."

Anxiously Coyote waited while the game went back, and then came toward him again. At the last throw, the ring hung briefly in midair, motionless; then shaking and spinning as if unable to decide, it began a slow descent to earth. The sticks thrown after it wavered in the sunshine, hesitant, and then fell without connecting, hiding the players momentarily in a cloud of dust. The ring rolled to Coyote. "Hurry granddaughter," he whispered, and seizing her in his mouth, he sped toward the hill.

As soon as the dust cleared the buffalo came thundering after him, but before they could catch Coyote, he reached Badger. Badger, taking the ring, quickly dug a hole and disappeared with it underground. Coyote followed him down. The buffalo trampled the ground around the hole, tearing up the earth with their horns. Coyote lay there trembling. "If they find me . . . oh, don't let them find me. . . ."

But it was the ring they wanted, not Coyote. When Badger came up with her in his mouth, the buffalo rushed off in his direction, and he had to go underground again. He kept digging tunnels and coming out, the buffalo running after him all the time and stopping to trample and tear up the ground wherever he disappeared.

Poor Badger! By the time he got to Wolf he was exhausted. Wearily he handed over the ring and, without a word, went underground to rest. Wolf, a very fast runner, left the buffalo far behind and was soon at the foot of the tree where Hawk waited. Dropping the ring on the ground in front of him, he sat down to catch his breath.

Hawk came down from his branch. "What's this ring? I thought there was a girl. . . . Where's Coyote?"

"I—don't—know," Wolf gasped, "but—here —she is." He pushed the ring over, but Hawk just stood there. "Well you can take her or not, whichever you please. It's up to you now. I'm too tired to argue." He crawled under some low bushes and was gone.

Hawk stared at the ring for a while, and then awkwardly put his head through it and slipped her around his neck. But when he tried to fly he discovered he couldn't. "Too heavy in front," he grumbled. "How can I carry this, anyway?" He pulled off the ring and arranged her in both of his claws. He could hear the buffalo coming closer. At last he got off, and after a long and tiring flight, he flapped gratefully into the shelter of Rusty-Blackbird's tree. The buffalo were catching up fast.

Waiting outside their lodge for Coyote, the brothers watched a familiar dust cloud begin to rise slowly in the distant hills.

"Buffalo are coming," observed the youngest, breaking their worried silence. "Will she be with them?" Of the four, he was closest to his sister.

"She will come." It was the second eldest

speaking. He was known for his wisdom, so they were comforted. "But I cannot say about Coyote," he added. Coyote puzzled even him.

The second youngest narrowed his eyes. "He said he would *surely* bring her today, didn't he? If not . . . ."

The boys stopped talking. Because the day was clear, it wasn't long before they were able to see the buffalo's huge, lowered heads, and they strained their eyes for some sign of the girl. Suddenly the youngest asked, "What's on that buffalo's head?"

The others crowded around him. "Can you see her? Which buffalo? Where?"

"There!" cried the eldest. "I see it too, but it isn't . . . ."

"It isn't? . . . Then what is it?"

"It's . . . ."

It was Rusty-Blackbird! Tired of flying, he had settled on the shaggy head of a bull. The ring, bouncing gaily around his neck, seemed to be enjoying the ride as much as he was! As for the buffalo, they were so intent on running after the ring that they never even looked up. They had no idea she was on her way home right along with them!

As the buffalo neared the lodge, Rusty-Blackbird saw the boys with their arrows aimed. "Don't shoot!" he shouted. "I've got your sister around my neck—don't shoot!" But in the confusion no one heard him, and when the brothers let their arrows go, they were startled to see the bird with the ring around its neck fly up over their lodge and down through the smoke-hole.

Inside, Rusty-Blackbird carefully set the ring by the fire. "Whew, that was close," he said to the ring. "Didn't you enjoy the ride—even though it was a little bumpy?" He wanted to be nice to her and when the ring made no answer, he felt somewhat embarrassed. "Well, I'm sure you'll be more comfortable here," he said backing off toward the door. "Now, if you'll excuse me, I'm going out to watch the fight."

But outside it was all over. Since the ring had vanished once more, the buffalo had turned around and were on their way home. The brothers were watching them disappear over the hills in the late afternoon.

"They came but she didn't come," said the youngest.

"You mean Coyote didn't bring her," the second youngest reminded. He looked grim.

"But *I* did," said Rusty-Blackbird proudly. He flew down from a branch and perched on the shoulder of the eldest brother. "She's safe inside," he announced, then warning as they all ran toward the lodge, "but she's been transformed into a ring."

"A ring!" The youngest rushed for the doorway but ran straight into his sister—or at least the girl in front of him looked exactly like her. "Are you my sister?" he asked hopefully.

The girl laughed and kissed him, and assured him that she was. Then she turned to Rusty-Blackbird, who was finding it hard to believe his eyes, though he did think she was pretty. "I became myself as soon as the buffalo left," she explained. "And I enjoyed the ride—even the bumpy part. Thank you for carrying me."

"But how come it was he who brought you?" asked one of the brothers. "What happened to Coyote? And why were you a ring?"

"I'll get Coyote," Rusty-Blackbird offered, "so he can tell you the story himself."

Coyote still lay in the very first hole Badger had dug.

"Coyote!" Rusty-Blackbird shouted down to him. "You can come out now. The buffalo are back in their own country and the girl has been returned to her brothers. Everything's all right."

"Well, I'm glad of that," said Coyote, not moving. "Because all I want to do is live in this nice, peaceful hole where there are no buffalo and no brothers to bother me."

"But you must come out, at least to thank those who helped you," Rusty-Blackbird insisted, "and the boys want to hear your story."

"All right, yes, all right." Grumbling, Coyote scrambled out into the waning daylight, squinting and looking dirtier than ever.

They first went to Badger, who also had remained underground. When they called him to come out, he shouted that he was perfectly satisfied where he was. "Those buffalo really frightened me," he complained, "so I dug in deep."

"You mean you can't get out?" asked Coyote.

"Not exactly," Badger answered, "but my claws have grown extremely long, and I think it might be better if I continue living in the ground."

Coyote agreed.

They found Wolf, who said he was leaving the country. He told them he had run so fast and in such a fright that he had no more desire to be near animals or people. He wanted to be away from *everybody*, and would make his home in the hills. With a parting glare at Coyote, he ran off.

"Now what about Hawk?" Rusty-Blackbird asked Coyote.

"Well what about Hawk?" Coyote asked back. Neither knew what to say to him; and they never found him, for he had flown as far away as he knew how, and was, ever after, only a tiny speck in the sky.

Rusty-Blackbird laughed. "To tell you the truth, I was the only one who had any fun." Suddenly he stopped. The sun had set and they were on their way back to the lodge. "I think I'll go the other way," he told Coyote. "I've just decided to return to buffalo country."

Coyote stared. "You're sure that buffalo ride didn't shake you up too much—or something?"

"But it will be good for me to live among them," Rusty-Blackbird explained. "I can rest on their backs when they sun themselves, or ride their heads when they run. And people will always remember when they see me with the buffalo . . ." He smoothed a wing feather and grinned at Coyote . . . "that it was *I* who brought the ring-girl to her brothers."

"Fine," said Coyote, who really didn't want to argue about it. "Just don't ask me to go along." But Rusty-Blackbird, his feathers arranged, was gone in the gathering dusk.

That night Coyote returned to the brothers. He told them how he had found their sister transformed into the ring the buffalo loved to play with, and how the other animals had helped him bring her back.

"But I knew I could *surely* get her back in one day," he said, glancing around at the brothers. "And now that she is home, I am satisfied." Though he wasn't really for he was still hungry, but felt it wasn't the time to ask. "I won't ever again try to hunt my own meat," he promised, and then added slyly, "but since you'll always have plenty, I'll just come here at night and steal yours!"

And so he went along. Ever since this time the other animals are wary of Coyote, and he never comes to a prairie lodge in the daytime, but only once in a while at night.

COYOTE CONQUERS THE IYA

One bright day Coyote wandered up a hill and at the top ran straight into Iya, the eater, who had come up the other side. Iya sucked people in with his powerful breath and could eat an entire tribe for one meal. Terrified, Coyote tried to run back down the hill but he couldn't. With every breath, the eater pulled him closer and closer to that enormous mouth.

"Oh no, I'm not going to die on a beautiful day like this, am I?" Coyote thought suddenly. He staggered around and finally managed to fling himself out of Iya's reach. Grabbing a handful of dust, he rubbed it hard into the outside of his thigh and on his backside. "Hope this works," he breathed, and approaching Iya as close as he dared, greeted him confidently. "Well, well, well, if it isn't my younger brother—er, um,—or is it my elder brother? Oh, brother! Which one of us is older anyway?"

Iya opened his mouth in Coyote's direction but said nothing.

Coyote struggled away and tried again. "Listen, little brother, uh—big brother—stand a little farther off, won't you? I mean, if you come any closer this way, I might draw you in with my breath—you know I could if I wanted to. . . ."

Though Iya didn't move or say anything, he kept on breathing, forcing Coyote to tear himself away once more. "Come on, younger brother . . . or whichever you are . . . older? Are you older? When were you born?"

"Why, I was born when this earth and this

sky were first made—of course I'm older than you."

Iya had spoken at last! Coyote clapped his hand over his mouth as though he were completely surprised. "Don't be silly," he replied. "I made this earth and sky myself, how could you . . ." He broke off, looking at Iya and pretending to think hard. "Oh, but *now* I remember! There was a little bit left over after I finished that I didn't know what to do with, so I wadded it all up and tossed it away. And that grew into little you, eh? Well, well, well, then I *am* your elder brother after all!"

Trying not to look nervous, Coyote waited for Iya's reply. Since everything about Iya was enormous except his brain, he believed the whole story and agreed, finally, that Coyote was the elder of the two; this meant he could give the orders. With a sigh of relief, Coyote approached Iya from the side. "Now then, little brother, where

are you going?" he asked, carefully shrinking away from the eater's breath. He was not as afraid as before, but felt he should be cautious. Stupid or not, Iya was still the eater.

"I'm going to that camp over there to have my dinner." Iya pointed in the direction from which Coyote had just come. "I'm going to eat the people," he said matter-of-factly. "I always do."

"Now isn't that something—you can tell we're really brothers!" Coyote reached out sideways to shake Iya's hand. "That's exactly where I'm going, too. We can go together!"

Iya had trouble walking because he was so heavy, so they traveled slowly, stopping often for him to rest. When they halted at nightfall, they were just nearing the camp. Iya lay down and soon fell asleep, his wide mouth open. Sneaking up carefully, Coyote peered in. There, within Iya's huge body, were all the people he had ever eaten! Each tribe had its own camp circle, and all of them

seemed perfectly content, living exactly as they had lived on earth.

Coyote blinked, rubbed his eyes, then looked again. He could hardly believe it. Even races and games were going on. For a while he watched a game of Dakota ball, then a group of dancers from the Men's Society performing around a circle. He saw hunters carrying game, and another group doing the White-Pack-Strap dance.

Completely fascinated, Coyote hung over the edge of Iya's mouth and nearly allowed himself to be pulled in. He was watching some women carry food to the council tipi, where the old men were sitting around eating and telling stories, when the eater stirred. Quickly Coyote withdrew, puzzled and frightened. "How can I trap him before he eats more people?" he wondered. He spent the night trying to figure it out, and when Iya awoke he was ready. "Little brother," he began as soon as Iya's eyes were open, "big as you are, is there any-thing at all that scares you?"

"Why do you want to know?" asked Iya suspiciously, turning his breath in Coyote's direction. He was still lying down.

Coyote jumped back behind Iya's ear. "I—I just thought I'd ask, in case I ever have to protect you, since you're my younger brother," he said, not sure at all that he sounded convincing.

But it didn't take much to convince Iya. He heaved his immense body into a sitting position. "To tell you the truth," he admitted, "I'm scared of the sound of rattles and drums. And hoot owls really give me the chills." He opened his mouth in a huge yawn that forced Coyote off his feet. "And now that I think of it, the sound of men shouting —now that's enough to scare me to death."

"Well it certainly is amazing how we brothers are alike!" Coyote said cheerfully, dusting himself off. "You know, little one, those are exactly the same things I'm afraid of?"

"Really?" asked Iya, somewhat bored by the conversation. He was hungry, and nothing else mattered. "I'm hun——"

"Oh yes," Coyote interrupted, "while you were asleep I had an idea. Since it's so hard for you to get around, why don't you stay here while I go on ahead to the camp?"

Iya frowned. "Those people are mine to eat," he said, looking ugly.

"Little brother, I wouldn't take your food," Coyote assured him. "I'll just mark the center tipi with a cross and come right back. Then we'll go to the camp together, and starting at each end, we can eat our way toward the middle. Whoever arrives at the marked tipi first gets to eat the other, and that will be his reward for winning!" Coyote put on his trickiest smile and let it rest there all over his face until he felt stiff.

Finally Iya reluctantly agreed. "Go ahead," he said, "but hurry . . . I'm hun——"

"Yes, I know you're hungry," called Coyote over his shoulder, for he was already off and running to the camp.

He entered shouting: "Attention, everyone! I have news for you so come listen! I have just played a trick on a very supernatural Iya, and that's why I'm here!"

People crowded around as he went on yelling: "When I asked him what he was afraid of, he told me rattles and drums, and owls hooting, and men shouting . . ."

"But is he on his way to eat us?" someone interrupted.

". . . . so hurry up," Coyote continued, ignoring the question, "for while he was sleeping I looked into Iya's mouth and saw thousands of people camped inside his body! All the tribes he has ever eaten! There are tipis with blue wind-flaps, and tipis with black wind-flaps, and a lot of

painted tipis. . . ."

Nobody was listening. They were all madly searching for rattles, trying to find drums. In a few minutes everyone was ready. Coyote led them to a place some distance from where Iya was waiting, hidden by a hill, and urged them to be quiet. "First give me a minute to get over this hill," he whispered.

The people waited silently until they felt sure he had arrived; then, hooting, shaking rattles, beating drums, and shouting, they charged the hill. Iya sat up, turning his head frantically from side to side, crazy with fear. He tried to rise but fell over with a great crash as the tribe surrounded him. They scared him to death with their shouting; and when that dangerous breath had stopped, they tore his body open to free those inside.

For one whole day people crawled out of Iya, moving themselves and all their belongings. Each tribe settled at a different bend of the river, and by nightfall, the cooking fires had been built. Everywhere along the river they sparkled like stars.

Now it is said that if Iya hadn't been destroyed he would surely have been eating the entire population, even to this day. So for once, before he went along, Coyote did something to deserve people's thanks.

Heha'yela owi'hake. There it ends.